Illustrator
Jose L. Tapia

Contributing Editor
Walter Kelly, M.A.

Editorial Project Manager
Karen Goldfluss, M.S. Ed.

Editor-in-Chief
Sharon Coan, M.S. Ed.

Art Director
Elayne Roberts

Associate Designer
Denise Bauer

Cover Artist
Sue Fullam

Product Manager
Phil Garcia

Imaging
David Bennett
Ralph Olmedo, Jr.

Publishers
Rachelle Cracchiolo, M.S. Ed.
Mary Dupuy Smith, M.S. Ed.

Activities for Any Literature Unit

Intermediate

Authors

Patsy Carey, Cynthia Holzschuher,
Susan Kilpatrick, John and Patty Carratello

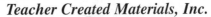

Teacher Created Materials, Inc.
6421 Industry Way
Westminster, CA 92683
www.teachercreated.com

©1996 Teacher Created Materials, Inc.
Reprinted, 2001
Made in U.S.A.
ISBN-1-57690-004-5

Teacher Created Materials

Table of Contents

Introduction

Good books can touch our lives like good friends. Within their pages are words and characters that can inspire us to achieve our highest ideals. We can turn to them for companionship, recreation, comfort, and guidance. They can also give us cherished stories to hold in our hearts forever.

With this in mind, *Activities for Any Literature Unit* has been designed for use with students in the intermediate grades. The lessons and projects may be used with a book you are reading with the class or be adapted to stories in your reading series. They are ideal for core literature and for partner and individualized reading. Even though students are reading different books, the same lesson can be applicable to all on a given day.

Ideas are developed to guide students in individualized as well as cooperative learning activities. There are eight sections:

- **Pre-reading Activities**
- **Reading Response Journals**
- **Vocabulary Ideas**
- **Book Report Ideas**
- **Graphic Organizers**
- **Multiple Intelligences**
- **Bloom's Taxonomy Activities**
- **Culminating Activity: "Q and A"** (adaptable to any book or story)

You will find generic activity sheets to provide simple and immediate instruction as well as creative ideas to address specific learning styles. The lessons are designed to teach and reinforce such skills as basic vocabulary, sequencing, and character and plot development.

Moreover, specific suggestions are supplied for assignments geared to each of Bloom's levels of learning—knowledge activities, comprehension activities, application activities, analysis activities, synthesis activities, and evaluation activities.

Special attention has also been paid to Howard Gardner's theory of multiple intelligences, leading to a series of suggested activities specially designed to appeal to each of seven types of intelligence.

It is the hope of the authors that *Activities for Any Literature Unit* will become an invaluable tool in simplifying your entire language curriculum.

Pre-reading Activities

Before you begin reading your literature selection with your students, do some pre-reading activities to stimulate interest and enhance comprehension. Here are some activities that might work for your class, depending on the specific book or story selected.

1. What have you heard about this novel? What information do you already know?

2. Predict what the story might be about just by looking at the cover illustration.

3. Discuss other books by the author that students may have heard about or read.

4. Respond to the following:

   ■ Are you interested in . . .

   • stories about characters who have to be heroic?

   • stories with adventure and life-or-death struggles?

   • stories dealing with a young person having experiences that make him/her grow up?

   • stories that show a young person is capable of making important decisions and taking action?

   • stories that have both funny and sad incidents?

   ■ Why might young boys or girls be forced to live on their own without anyone taking care of them?

   ■ How can unusual occurrences change a young person's life?

   ■ What is it like being in a new and completely different environment?

5. Work in groups to create a factual and/or fictional story about a child who has exciting and strange adventures.

6. Write descriptions or brainstorm ideas about what makes a person strong or courageous.

7. Use a picture to introduce the literature selection to your class. The picture can also be used as a journal cover for reading response journals or as the centerpiece of a bulletin board display of student work. After the story has been completed, the picture may be used to stimulate discussion about the ending of the story.

Reading Response Journals

One excellent way to ensure that the reading of literature becomes a personal experience for each student is to include the use of reading response journals in your plans. In these journals, students can be encouraged to respond to the story in a number of ways. Here are a few ideas.

- Tell them that the purpose of the journal is to record their thoughts, ideas, observations, and questions as they read.

- Provide students with, or ask them to suggest, topics from the story that would stimulate writing. Specific examples of the following might serve as examples:

  - situations provoking strong emotions, such as anger, fear, or great admiration
  - situations which are ambiguous, unclear, or cause puzzlement and wonder
  - conditions, occupations, or subjects about which they like to know more, such as life at sea, veterinary work, crafts, electronics, flying, space—anything personally engaging an interest

- After the reading of each chapter, students can write one or more new things they learned in the chapter.

- Have students use a double-entry journal by writing one short quote that interests them from each chapter on the left of their paper. On the right side they should express their own ideas about the quote.

- Ask students to draw their responses to certain events or characters in the story, using blank pages in their journals.

- Tell students that they may use their journals to record "diary-type" responses that they may want to enter.

- Give students quotes from the novel and ask them to write their own responses. Make sure to do this before you go over the quotations in class. In groups they could list the different ways students can respond to the same quote.

- Allow students time to write in their journals daily.

- Personal reflections will be read by the teacher, but no corrections or letter grades will be assigned. Credit is given for effort, and all students who sincerely try will be awarded credit. If a grade is desired for this type of entry, grade according to the number of journal entries completed. For example, if five journal assignments were made and the student conscientiously completes all five, then he or she receives an "A."

- Nonjudgmental teacher responses should be made to let the students know you enjoy their journals. Here are some types of responses that will please your journal writers and encourage them to write more.

  - *"You have really found what's important in the story!"*
  - *"You write so clearly, I almost feel as if I am there."*
  - *"If you feel comfortable, I'd like you to share this with the class. I think they'll enjoy it as much as I have."*

Vocabulary Activities

You can help your students learn and retain the vocabulary in the literature selection by providing them with interesting vocabulary activities. Here are some ideas to try.

- People of all ages like to make and solve puzzles. Ask your students to make their own **crossword puzzles** or **word search puzzles** using the vocabulary words from the story.

- Challenge your students to a **vocabulary bee!** This is similar to a spelling bee, but in addition to spelling each word correctly, the game participants must correctly define the words as well.

- Play **vocabulary concentration.** The goal of this game is to match vocabulary words with their definitions. Divide the class into groups of two to five students. Have students make two sets of the cards the same size and color. On one set have them write the vocabulary words. On the second set have them write the definitions. All cards are mixed together and placed face down on a table. A player picks two cards. If the pair matches the word with its definition, the player keeps the cards and takes another turn. If the cards do not match, they are returned to their places face down on the table, and another player takes a turn. Players must concentrate to remember the locations of the words and their definitions. The game continues until all matches have been made. This is an ideal activity for free exploration time.

- Have your students practice their writing skills by creating sentences and paragraphs in which multiple vocabulary words are used correctly. Ask them to share their **compact vocabulary** sentences and paragraphs with the class.

- Ask your students to create paragraphs which use the vocabulary words to present **history lessons** that relate to the time period of the novel.

- Challenge your students to use a specific vocabulary word from the story at least **10 times in one day.** They must keep a record of when, how, and why the word was used.

- As a group activity, have students work together to create an **illustrated dictionary** of the vocabulary words.

- Play **20 clues** with the entire class. In this game, one student selects a vocabulary word and gives clues about this word, one by one, until someone in the class can guess the word.

- Play **vocabulary charades.** In this game, vocabulary words are acted out.

Vocabulary Activities *(cont.)*

Following are some additional suggestions to add to the previous page. Students can begin with the contextual vocabulary from the literature selections and build upon them to use strategies for retaining, using, and extending their knowledge of word meanings. You may find some of these activities useful:

- Have students **illustrate the vocabulary words** on one side of a sheet of paper. The word is written on the back. These can be used as a "quiz show" for a whole-class activity, with one student acting as moderator, or they can be placed on a bulletin board or hallway display with the words added at the bottom. As a variation, students may do impromptu drawings on the chalkboard, challenging classmates to guess the word.

- **Language experience is fun at any age.** Give each student a card with one of the vocabulary words on it. Allow a few minutes of "think time" for him/her to make up a sentence using that vocabulary word correctly. If you are teaching plot sequence, you may direct students to concentrate on retelling the narrative; for an enrichment activity, students could be given a general topic and an idea of sequence for an original story. It helps to tape responses for later transcription or student dictation.

- Help students to **experiment with word histories.** Discuss specific words with the class, ones that you know contain foreign language roots. Make sure that these words have at least eight related words in the dictionary. Explain that related words use a common root but differ in their prefixes or suffixes. Have students illustrate their expanded vocabulary using a word web.

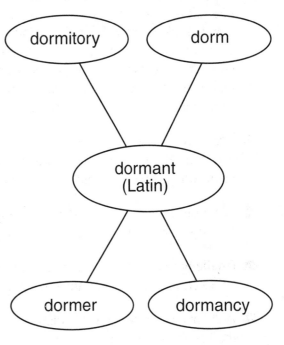

- **Play password.** Have the group divide into two teams. Have vocabulary words already prepared, with each written on a 3" x 5" (7.5 cm x 12.5 cm) index card. One student from each team is to give clues using only one word and having a 30-second time limit for response. Allow the student with the correct response to become the clue giver, and keep score by allotting 10 points for a correct answer on the first clue, nine points on the second clue, etc.

- **Use suffixes** to teach grammar. Since many suffixes actually give clues to parts of speech, have students categorize words as usually nouns, verbs, adjectives, or adverbs. For instance, a word that ends in *-ment* or *-tion* is usually a noun; a word that ends in *-ly* is usually an adverb; and a word that ends in *-ed* or *-ing* is usually a verb or an adjective (participle). A little time spent with a dictionary may help students to apply grammar concepts more confidently and precisely.

- Have students **locate the vocabulary word in the story.** Proceed to have them guess the meaning by using context clues.

Book Report Activities

There are many ways to report on a book. After you have finished reading the literature selection, choose one method of reporting that interests you. It may be a way your teacher suggests, an idea of your own, or one of the ways mentioned below.

■ **See What I Read?**

This report is visual. A model of a scene from the story can be created, or a likeness of one or more of the characters from the story can be drawn or sculpted.

■ **Time Capsule**

This report provides people living in the future with the reasons your story or book is such an outstanding book. Make a time-capsule design and neatly print or write your reasons inside the capsule. You may wish to "bury" your capsule after you have shared it with your classmates. Perhaps one day someone will find it and read your selection because of what you wrote.

■ **Act It Out!**

This report lends itself to a group project. A size-appropriate group prepares a scene from the story for dramatization, acts it out, and relates the significance of the scene to the entire book. Costumes and props will add to the dramatization.

■ **Who or What?**

This report is similar to "20 Questions." The reporter gives a series of clues about a character from the story in vague-to-precise, general-to-specific order. After all clues have been given, the identity of the mystery character must be deduced. After the character has been identified, the same reporter presents another 20 clues about an event in the story.

■ **Dress 'n' Guess!**

Come to class dressed as one of the characters. Tell the class your version of the story from that character's perspective. Act like that character, and answer any questions the class may have about you and your life.

■ **Sales Talk**

This report serves as an advertisement to "sell" your selection to one or more specific groups. You decide on the group to target and the sales pitch you will use. Include some kind of graphics in your presentation.

■ **Literary Interview**

This report is done in pairs. One student will pretend to be a character in the story, steeped completely in the persona of his or her character. The other student will play the role of a television or radio interviewer, trying to provide the audience with insights into the character's personality and life. It is the responsibility of the partners to create meaningful questions and appropriate responses.

■ **Historical**

Consider one of your interests. Research the way that interest or a related one was interpreted in the year the story is set. Report to the class. Some possible topics are food, entertainment, transportation, politics, and lives of the people.

Book Report Activities *(cont.)*

After you finish reading your story, choose one of the following methods of reporting that interests you. If you have an idea of your own, ask your teacher if you may do that instead.

■ **Pen Pal**

Write a letter to one of the characters in your story. Tell him/her how similar and different your life is to his/hers. Ask that character questions and offer your opinions about some of the situations in the story. Then write a letter back to yourself pretending to be that character.

■ **The Funny Papers**

Make a comic strip about one of the scenes in your story. Include a title frame and lots of conversation bubbles to retell what happened.

■ **TV Commercial**

Write a TV commercial for the book and present it live to the class. Or, produce a commercial on a videotape and bring it in for viewing.

■ **Talk Show Host/Hostess**

Pretend that you are a television talk show host/hostess and will be interviewing a character from your story. Compose a list of questions that your viewers would be interested in. Ask one of your friends to be the character and conduct a "live taping" of your show or produce a video.

■ **Movie Marquee**

Your story is about to become a major movie, and you have been chosen to design the promotional poster! Include the title, author of the book, a listing of the major characters in the book and the actors and actresses who will play them, and a short paragraph summarizing the story.

■ **Mobile Magic**

Create and assemble an exciting and colorful mobile to display in your classroom. Using a coat hanger, string or fishing wire, and heavy paper, show the plot, setting, and characters of your story. Start by placing the setting at the top level, the characters at the middle level, and developing the plot at the bottom level.

■ **Mystery Box Game**

Cover a shoe box with construction paper and color large question marks all over the box. On one side of the box, write the title of the book. Fill your box with five objects that are related to your story. Allow the class time to ask "yes or no" questions about the objects. When someone correctly guesses the object, he or she will need to explain how the object relates to the story.

■ **Patchwork Quilt**

Use a piece of 18" x 26" (46 cm x 66 cm) tagboard and six 8" x 8" (20 cm x 20 cm) squares of paper. Glue the squares on the tagboard and simulate "stitching" around each piece using a crayon or marker. Each of the squares will tell specific information about your story. One square should state the title and author, and the other squares should tell about the characters, plot, and settings.

■ **Board Game**

Create a board game using vocabulary, information, and characters from your story. Be sure to include instructions that tell the rules and object of the game. Make game pieces and cards.

Graphic Organizers

■ Many Different Kinds

Graphic organizers are diagrams, sketches, pictures, clusters, maps, outlines, etc., designed to help students put their thoughts into a logical form in order to clarify concepts or point out relationships between and among them. There are as many graphic organizers as there are people who organize. Some, however, have become more generally accepted than others.

Teachers who are trying to get students to write a paragraph with a main idea and four supporting ideas might draw a picture on the board, depending on their degree of artistic prowess, of an elephant or of a table. The body of the elephant (or the top of the table) is the main idea and the legs are the supporting ideas. The elephant, or the table, stands up best when all the ideas are present. For example:

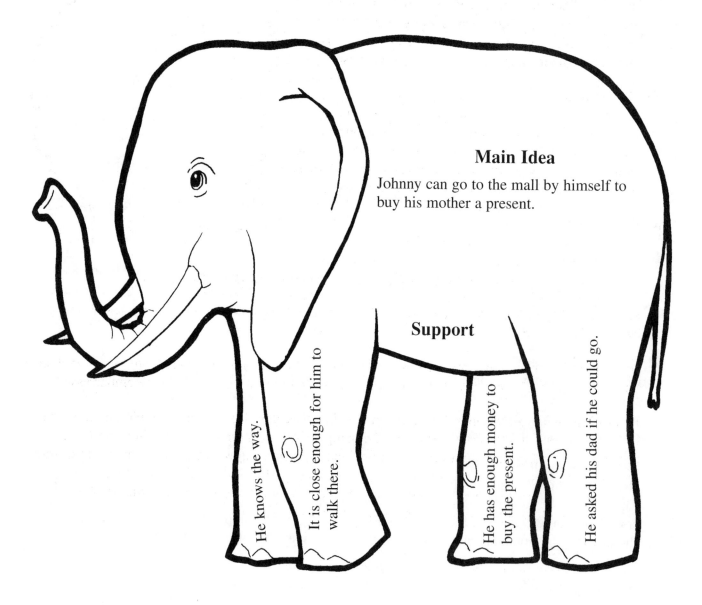

Main Idea

Johnny can go to the mall by himself to buy his mother a present.

Support

He knows the way.

It is close enough for him to walk there.

He has enough money to buy the present.

He asked his dad if he could go.

You probably draw items like this on the board all the time. In so doing, you are using graphic organizers.

Graphic Organizers *(cont.)*

■ Formal Outlines

The more traditional organizers are still valuable. Formal outlines, for example, have been around for many years. They have recently lost favor, being replaced in many cases by more symbolic representations of thought, but they are still useful for many people.

If a student thinks in outline form, he or she should be given the advantage of knowing how to write one. In many cases, outlines have been entirely replaced by clustering and mapping. Although these are valuable techniques, they may not show the relationships between ideas as clearly as an outline.

■ Venn Diagrams

Venn diagrams appear as two-, three-, and four-circle overlaps. They are introduced in some texts as early as second grade. Children seem to enjoy organizing their thoughts with these diagrams, and many social studies and math concepts can be clarified with their use.

■ The Open Mind

A line drawing of a head is one of the newer graphic organizers. Called the "open mind," it can symbolize the head of the student who is using it and offer a place to express his or her thoughts. Or it can symbolize the head (and thoughts) of a character in a story being read.

■ Possible Drawbacks

Graphic organizers are a long overdue gift to the visual and kinesthetic learner, but like many reforms, they carry with them the possibility for destroying the good things that already exist.

Students who think on a more abstract level like to put things into words, not pictures, in many cases.

In addition, some students are not sure of their ability to draw anything they would want to share with a group. They may need the technique but refuse to use it because they are embarrassed.

Finally, the ability to use graphic organizers, which were developed to help people think, is now being tested as a skill in itself. Students are being evaluated on their expertise in using these organizers, in addition to being evaluated on their understanding of the concepts these organizers were designed to help them understand. As educators, perhaps we need to think through our assessment priorities. It is important for teachers to determine the objective of the graphic organizer and its place in the assessment process before using it.

■ Do It Yourself

A selection of graphic organizers is provided on pages 12–17.

Graphic Organizers *(cont.)*

Cluster A

This type of graphic organizer places the main idea at its center, with supporting ideas radiating from the main idea.

- -

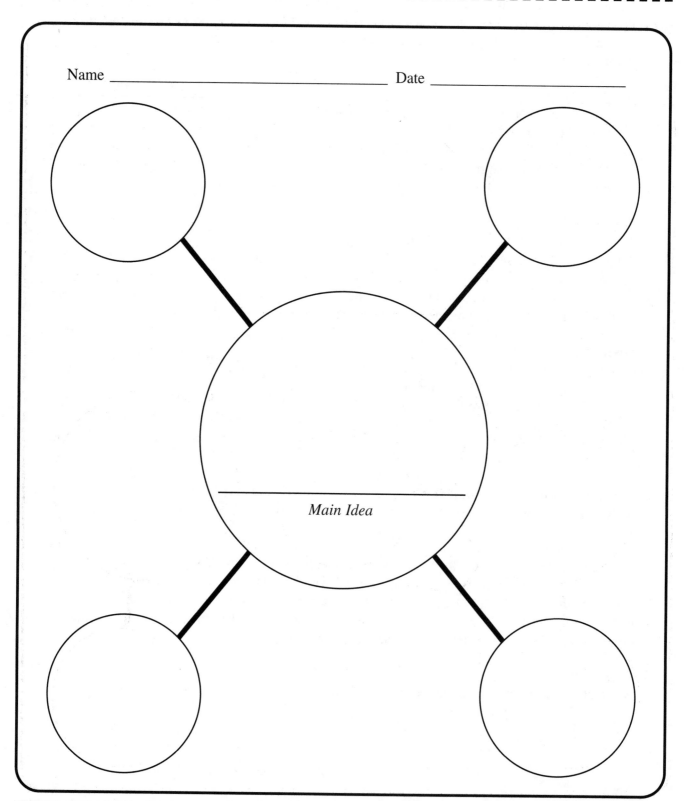

Name _____ Date _____

Main Idea

Graphic Organizers *(cont.)*

Cluster B

This is a variation of the cluster on page 12 with information clustered around the supporting ideas that connect to the main idea.

- -

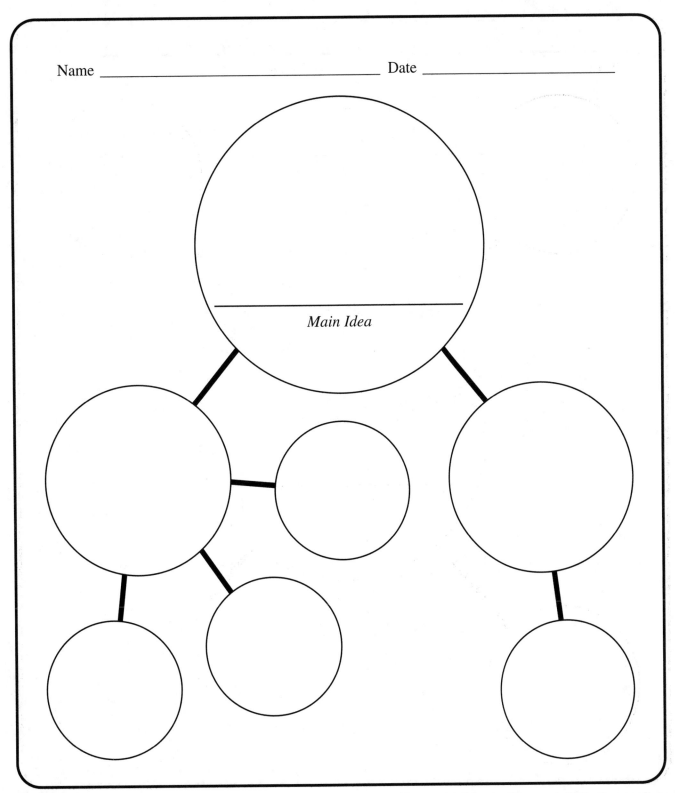

Name _____   Date _____

Main Idea

Graphic Organizers *(cont.)*

Venn Diagram A

A Venn diagram can show students' thought processes as they compare objects, demonstrating the differences and similarities which the objects possess. Areas where the circles overlap represent similar qualities between or among the objects. Areas of the circles which do not overlap should describe dissimilar characteristics.

- -

Name _____ Date _____

_____
Subject or Title

Graphic Organizers *(cont.)*

Venn Diagram B

A Venn diagram can show students' thought processes as they compare objects, demonstrating the differences and similarities which the objects possess. Areas where the circles overlap represent similar qualities between or among the objects. Areas of the circles which do not overlap should describe dissimilar characteristics. This Venn diagram is drawn to compare and contrast three objects.

Name _____ Date _____

_____

Subject or Title

Graphic Organizers *(cont.)*

Character Web

A character web is a design of boxes and circles which helps to analyze the basic attributes of a single character and his/her relationship to the book as a whole. A drawing and/or the name of the character goes in the middle box. It is surrounded by circles for specific characteristics such as physical description, personality traits, occupation/special abilities, and relationship to other characters. This is an excellent device to help understand and remember the characters in any story.

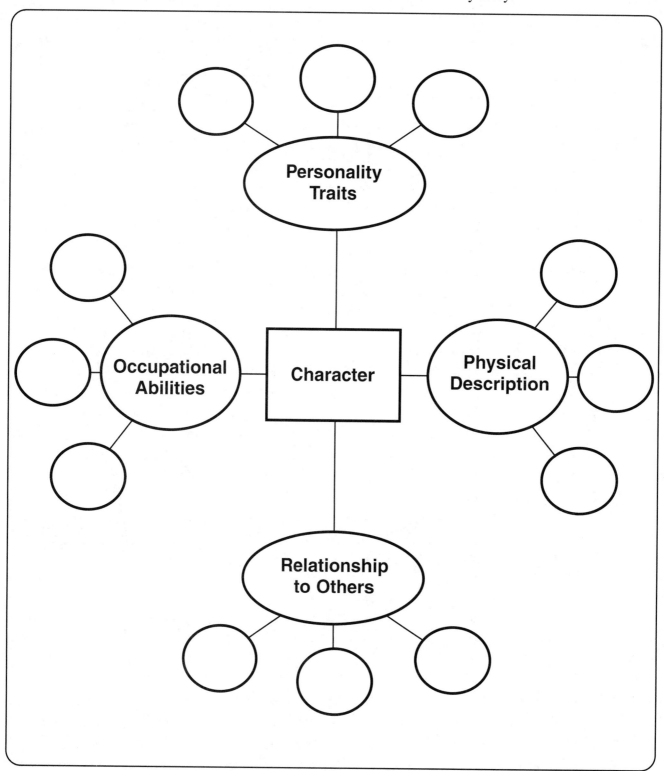

Graphic Organizers *(cont.)*

The Open Mind

Students write and organize their ideas inside the outline of the head, which symbolizes a character's thoughts.

Name _____ Date _____

Character

Multiple Intelligences

Howard Gardner's theory of multiple intelligences is well known but often difficult to incorporate into our lesson plans. Below is a review of Gardner's ideas as stated in *Frames of Mind*, 1985, along with a possible activity for each. They might make appropriate extra-credit assignments for your class.

Type of Learning	Activity
Linguistic: sensitivity to the meaning of words, to the grammar of language; ability to use language to convince others, to use language to remember; prefers written decisions to reading a map; thinks in words.	Assign these students to work on explaining any dialect or special terms used in your literature selection.
Logical-Mathematical: ability to manipulate numerical quantities, symbols, and operations; tends to be questioning and curious; likely to have solid rationales for decisions; looks for patterns, relationships.	Assign these students to report on what they feel is hard to understand or rationalize in the actions of the characters in the literature selection.
Spatial: ability to image; ability to rotate objects in the mind's eye; can read maps, graphs; learn through rhythm, rhyme, and pattern.	Assign this group to research art of the period and report to the class. Look for information on drawings, maps, or graphs to create for the literature selection.
Musical: sensitivity to music and sound; can learn through rhythm, rhyme, and pattern.	Assign students to research music of the period. Parts may be presented, sung, or performed in class if appropriate.
Bodily-Kinesthetic: ability to use one's body skillfully and expressively with great control; can learn through drama, movement, and touch.	Have these students dramatize a scene from the literature selection.
Intrapersonal: ability to examine one's own feelings; intuitive, works best on one's own in privacy; self-motivating.	These students can help the class to understand motivation in the literature selection. They may want to work alone; if so, give each a different section.
Interpersonal: ability to read the intentions, motivations, and temperaments of others; empathetic to others; charismatic leader; counselor, teacher; learns best through interaction, cooperation.	As a group, these students will help the class to understand the changing relationships of characters to one another.

Bloom's Taxonomy Activities

On the following three pages are 40 specific literature activities listed in rising levels of difficulty, skill development, and critical thinking. These may be adapted to different types of literature, as well as providing the teacher with flexible types of activities to match the differing abilities, needs, and aspirations of students in the modern classroom. Such an overall scope and framework allows the teacher to plan with assurance that all students are provided with activities designed to develop the full range of their cognitive abilities.

Knowledge

This level provides the student an opportunity to recall fundamental facts and information about the story. Success at this level will be evidenced by the student's ability to . . .

- **Match** character names with pictures of the characters.

- **Identify** the main characters in a crossword puzzle.

- **Match** statements with the characters who said them.

- **List** the main characteristics of one of the main characters in a WANTED poster.

- **Arrange** scrambled story pictures in sequential order.

- **Arrange** scrambled story sentences in sequential order.

- **Recall** details about the setting by creating a picture of where a part of the story took place.

Comprehension

This level provides the student an opportunity to demonstrate a basic understanding of the story. Success at this level will be evidenced by the student's ability to . . .

- **Interpret** pictures of scenes from the story.

- **Explain** selected ideas or parts from the story in his or her own words.

- **Draw** a picture showing what happened before and after a passage or illustration found in the book.

- **Predict** what could happen next in the story before the reading of the entire book is completed.

- **Construct** a pictorial time line which summarizes what happens in the story.

- **Explain** how the main character felt at the beginning, middle, and/or end of the story.

Bloom's Taxonomy Activities

(cont.)

Application

This level provides the student an opportunity to use information from the story in a new way. Success at this level will be evidenced by the student's ability to . . .

- **Classify** the characters as human, animal, or thing.

- **Transfer** a main character to a new setting.

- **Make** finger puppets and act out a part of the story.

- **Select** a meal that one of the main characters would enjoy eating; plan a menu, and a method of serving it.

- **Think** of a situation that occurred to a character in the story and write about how he or she would have handled the situation differently.

- **Give** examples of people the student knows who have the same problems as the characters in the story.

Analysis

This level provides the student an opportunity to take parts of the story and examine these parts carefully in order to better understand the whole story. Success at this level will be evidenced by the student's ability to . . .

- **Identify** general characteristics (stated and/or implied) of the main characters.

- **Distinguish** what could happen from what couldn't happen in the story in real life.

- **Select** parts of the story that were funniest, saddest, happiest, and most unbelievable.

- **Differentiate** fact from opinion.

- **Compare and/or contrast** two of the main characters.

- **Select** an action of a main character that was exactly the same as something the student would have done.

Bloom's Taxonomy Activities

(cont.)

Synthesis

This level provides the student with opportunity to put parts from the story together in a new way to form a new idea or product. Success at this level will be evidenced by the student's ability to . . .

- **Write** three new titles for the story that would give a good idea what it is about.

- **Create** a poster to advertise the story so people will want to read it.

- **Create** a new product related to the story.

- **Restructure** the roles of the main characters to create new outcomes in the story.

- **Compose** and perform a dialogue or monologue that will communicate the thoughts of the main characters at a given point in the story.

- **Imagine** that he or she is one of the main characters and write a diary account of daily thoughts and activities.

- **Create** an original character and tell how the character would fit into the story.

- **Write** the lyrics and music to a song that one of the main characters would sing if he/she became a rock star—and then perform it.

Evaluation

This level provides the student with an opportunity to form and present an opinion backed by sound reasoning. Success at this level will be evidenced by the student's ability to . . .

- **Decide** which character in the selection he or she would most like to spend a day with and why.

- **Judge** whether or not a character should have acted in a particular way and why.

- **Decide** if the story really could have happened and justify the decision.

- **Consider** how this story can help the student in his or her own life.

- **Appraise** the value of the story.

- **Compare** the story with another one the student has read.

- **Write** a recommendation as to why the book (story) should be read or not.

Finding Facts

Think about the local area, as well as the country and continent in which the action of your story takes place. Working with a partner or team, find out 20 facts about the setting of your story. List them below.

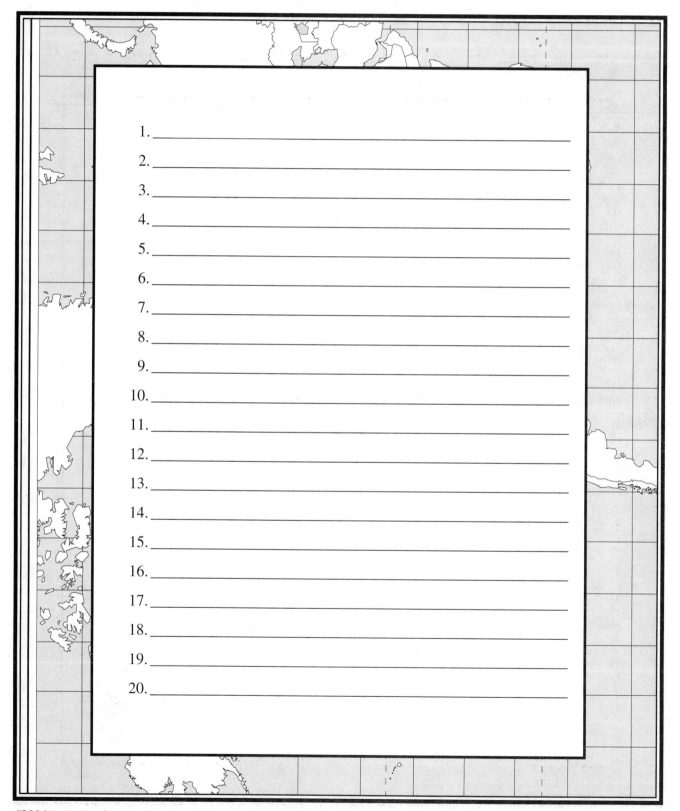

1. _____
2. _____
3. _____
4. _____
5. _____
6. _____
7. _____
8. _____
9. _____
10. _____
11. _____
12. _____
13. _____
14. _____
15. _____
16. _____
17. _____
18. _____
19. _____
20. _____

Mapping the Matter

Think about the places where the events occur in your story. In the space below, draw a map of the area and indicate where and when the important events took place. (*Note*: The events may all have taken place within a building, a small town, a large city, or even across a whole country or continent.) Make your map fit the events of your story.

Mapping the Matter *(cont.)*

Your teacher will list some places mentioned in the story you read. Locate those places on this map. Draw dotted lines on the map to show the routes taken by any characters your teacher names.

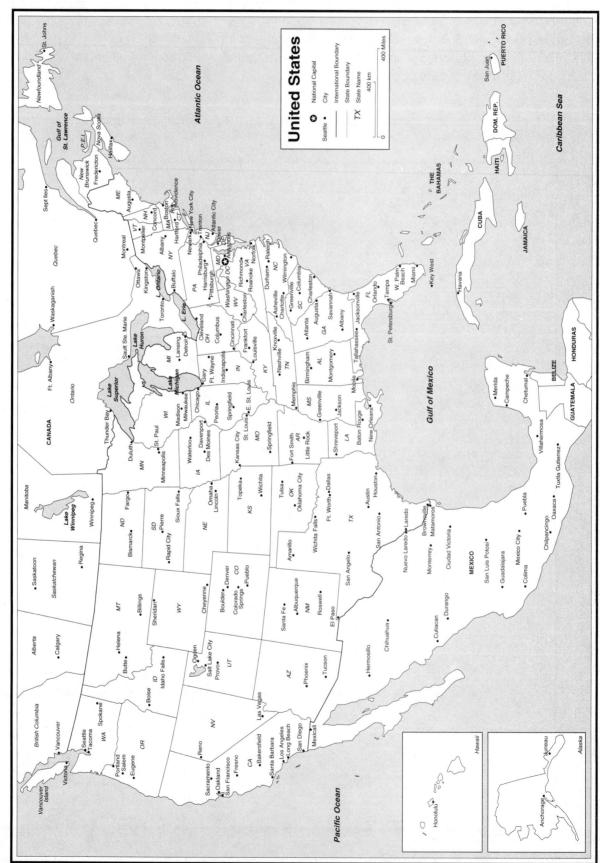

Mapping the Matter (cont.)

Your teacher will list some places mentioned in the story you read. Locate those places on this map. Draw dotted lines on the map to show the routes taken by any characters your teacher names.

3000 Km
3000 Mi.
Scale at the Equator.

Match These!

List below the names of five characters from your story. In the boxes on the right hand side of the diagram, write brief but accurate descriptions of each of those characters. DO NOT write the descriptions in the correct order. (On the back of the page, show an answer key for your work.) Now, exchange your work with someone else who has read the same book. See how well you have described the characters and how well your friend has read the story.

Character	Description
1. _____	a.
2. _____	b.
3. _____	c.
4. _____	d.
5. _____	e.

Who Said That?

Note to the teacher: *Fill the balloons with the quotations you wish the students to identify. On the next page, leave the balloons blank but fill in the character names. (This activity may be raised in difficulty, of course, simply by asking the student to write in the correct character name next to each balloon below.)* Cut out the word balloons. Match them with the characters who said them by pasting them in the proper spaces on the next page.

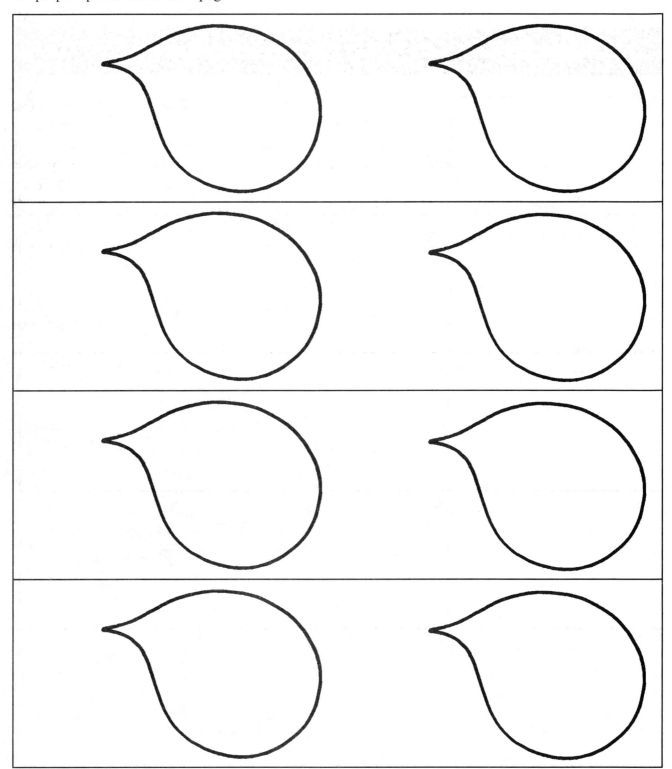

Who Said That? *(cont.)*

Paste the word balloons cut out from the previous page next to the correct character names shown in the spaces below.

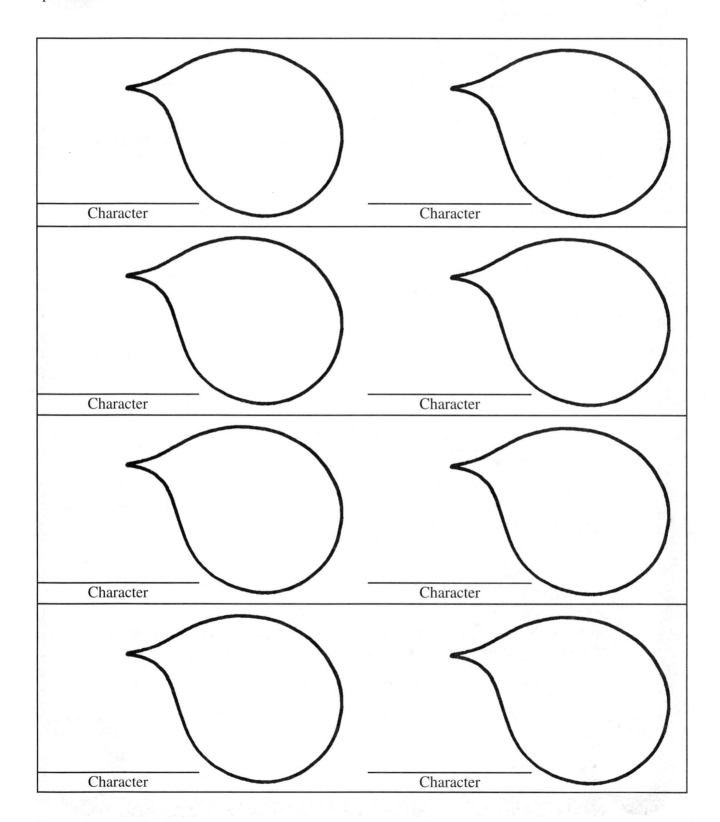

Wanted!

Make a "wanted" poster for one or more of the characters in the story you read.

Directions:

1. Use the Wanted! poster blank on the following page.
2. Draw a picture of your character in the rectangle.
3. Write the character's name under the picture.
4. List things that will help identify your character by filling in the blanks on the poster. Practice below; then, after your teacher checks your work, recopy the information neatly onto the poster.

Wanted for: (Your character might be wanted for having done something bad—or for something GOOD!)

_____

_____

_____

Description: (Name specific details like the following—height, weight, eye color, hair color, skin color, special marks like scars or tattoos, bald, hairy, special habits of talking or walking.)

_____

_____

_____

_____

Last seen: (Exactly when and where was your character last seen, and what was he/she doing? Was he/she with any known associates?)

_____

_____

_____

Reward: (What is the reward [money or special prize] for finding, capturing, or providing information leading to the capture of the wanted character?)

_____

_____

Wanted!

_____

Name

Wanted for: _____

Description: _____

Height_____ Weight_____

Eye color _____ Hair color_____ Skin color _____

Special marks _____

Special habits _____

Other details _____

Last seen: _____

_____

Reward: _____

Sequence of Events

Note to the teacher: *On the top set of blank strips below, write a series of events from your story in jumbled sequence. Have the students cut them out and paste them in correct order.*

Directions: Cut out the strips below and paste them in the order they occurred in the story.

_____

Name of Book or Story

Jumbled Order

A.

B.

C.

D.

E.

F.

G.

H.

I.

J.

Correct Order

1.

2.

3.

4.

5.

6.

7.

8.

9.

10.

Order, Please!

Note to the teacher: *In the spaces below, sketch or use stick figures to depict six events in your story in random order. (You might vary this by asking students to draw specific separate events, not mentioning their sequence. Later, have different students put the scenes in order.)*

Below are six things that happen in your story. Number them in the order they take place.

And Then . . .

You have just finished reading pages_____. They have ended with the following lines:

_____

_____

_____

What do you think will happen next? Write your ideas for the next episode in the story. Give your episode a title.

Title

_____

_____

_____

_____

_____

_____

_____

_____

_____

_____

_____

_____

_____

_____

_____

_____

Can You Guess?

Step 1   Select a character from your story or book.

Step 2   Fill in the following sentence clues about your chosen character.

Clue #1: If I were to tell you how my character looks, I would say that . . .

Name

_____

_____

_____

Clue #2: Something my character did was . . .

_____

_____

_____

Clue #3: Something my character said was . . .

_____

_____

_____

Clue #4: I think the story could/could not (circle one) have happened without my character because . . .

_____

_____

_____

Step 3   Read one clue at a time to the class. At the end of each clue, see if anyone can identify your character. If no one can guess correctly after the last clue, you may tell the class the name of your character.

Time Line

Note to the teacher: *In random order, fill the blank sentence strips below with events from your book or story. Alternatively, have students describe one event each within a sentence strip. Use their descriptions in random order to place below.*

Using the events listed below, construct a time line of story events. Do this by placing the event letters in the proper space on the time line.

A.

B.

C.

D.

E.

F.

G.

H.

I.

J.

Time Line of Events

1 →　2 →　3 →　4 →　5 →　6 →　7 →　8 →　9 →　10 →

How Do You Feel?

Pretend you are the following character in your story:

character	story

In your own words, explain how you felt at the following times:

At the beginning of the story . . .

In the middle of the story . . .

At the end of the story . . .

One-Pager

A "one-pager" is a chance for you to draw or write your reaction to your story or book. You may choose to do whatever you want on one page, as long as it relates to your story. You will need to decide whether your page should be all lined, have just a few lines, or have no lines at all.

The only requirement is that your page must have some color. If you do not want to draw, then put a colorful border around your writing.

Suggestions

- You can pick out a favorite quotation and illustrate it with your own view of the character(s).

- You can draw a scene that the author described in words.

- You can draw the climactic scene of the story.

- You can draw a scene that "occurs" before the action of the story.

- You can draw a scene that "occurs" after the story ends.

- You can draw a new book cover for the story.

- You can write your feelings about the story. For example, how does the story relate to the real world?

- You can write a review of the novel.

- You can draw a pictorial time line, summarizing what happens in the story.

Meals and Menus

Characters in literature differ in many ways—speech, actions, habits, clothing, and favorite foods. It is important that we eat the right amounts and the right kinds of foods every day. In that way we keep our bodies healthier and stronger. Study the chart below. It shows the kinds of foods one should eat each day and the number of servings one should have.

The world is a multicultural marvel, and books and stories bring that world close to us. Besides language and dress, one of the great signposts of a culture is its distinct preparation of food. The United States being a multicultural society, the American Dietetic Association has developed the three cultural food pyramids found on pages 39 to 40 to supplement the one below.

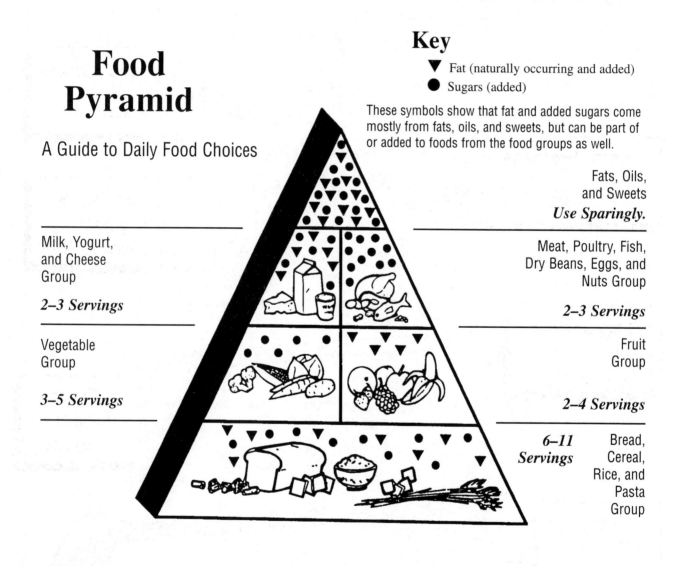

Food Pyramid

A Guide to Daily Food Choices

Milk, Yogurt, and Cheese Group

2–3 Servings

Vegetable Group

3–5 Servings

Key

▼ Fat (naturally occurring and added)
● Sugars (added)

These symbols show that fat and added sugars come mostly from fats, oils, and sweets, but can be part of or added to foods from the food groups as well.

Fats, Oils, and Sweets
Use Sparingly.

Meat, Poultry, Fish, Dry Beans, Eggs, and Nuts Group

2–3 Servings

Fruit Group

2–4 Servings

6–11 Servings — Bread, Cereal, Rice, and Pasta Group

What kinds of foods do you eat each day?

Do you eat vegetables? _____   Do you eat fruit? _____

Do you eat yogurt? _____   Do you eat cereal? _____

On the back of this paper, list other foods you usually eat each day.

Meals and Menus (cont.)

Chinese Fare

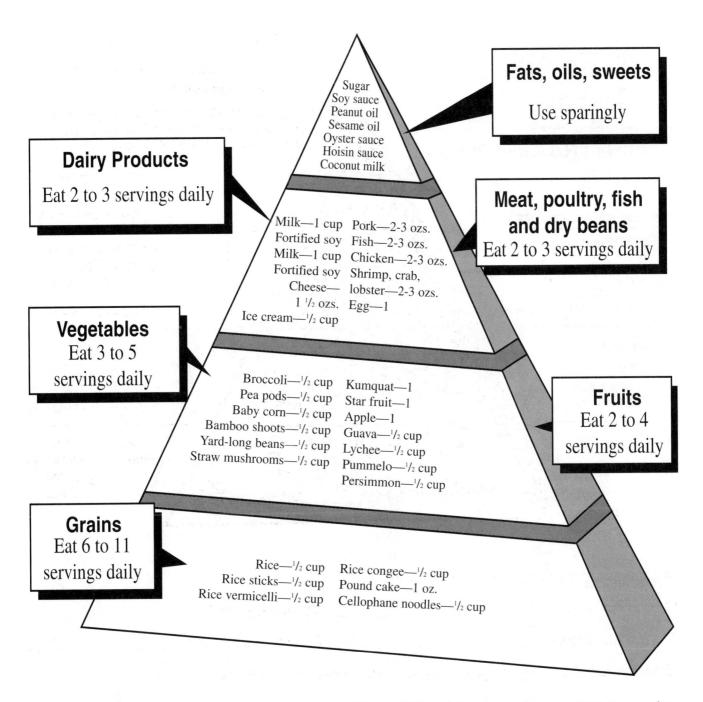

Fats, oils, sweets

Use sparingly

Sugar
Soy sauce
Peanut oil
Sesame oil
Oyster sauce
Hoisin sauce
Coconut milk

Dairy Products

Eat 2 to 3 servings daily

Meat, poultry, fish and dry beans
Eat 2 to 3 servings daily

Milk—1 cup   Pork—2-3 ozs.
Fortified soy   Fish—2-3 ozs.
Milk—1 cup   Chicken—2-3 ozs.
Fortified soy   Shrimp, crab,
Cheese—   lobster—2-3 ozs.
1 ¹/₂ ozs.   Egg—1
Ice cream—¹/₂ cup

Vegetables
Eat 3 to 5
servings daily

Broccoli—¹/₂ cup   Kumquat—1
Pea pods—¹/₂ cup   Star fruit—1
Baby corn—¹/₂ cup   Apple—1
Bamboo shoots—¹/₂ cup   Guava—¹/₂ cup
Yard-long beans—¹/₂ cup   Lychee—¹/₂ cup
Straw mushrooms—¹/₂ cup   Pummelo—¹/₂ cup
Persimmon—¹/₂ cup

Fruits
Eat 2 to 4
servings daily

Grains
Eat 6 to 11
servings daily

Rice—¹/₂ cup   Rice congee—¹/₂ cup
Rice sticks—¹/₂ cup   Pound cake—1 oz.
Rice vermicelli—¹/₂ cup   Cellophane noodles—¹/₂ cup

Meals and Menus *(cont.)*

Italian Fare

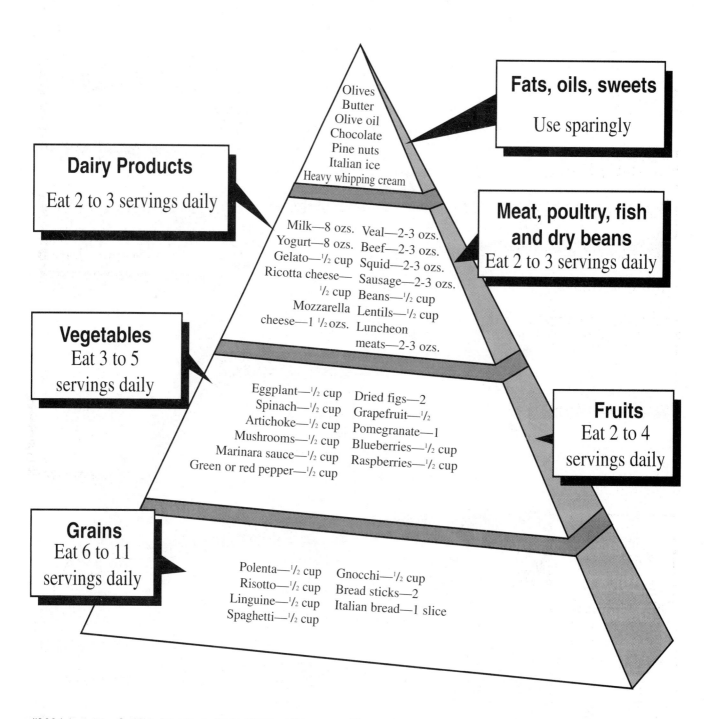

Fats, oils, sweets
Use sparingly

Olives
Butter
Olive oil
Chocolate
Pine nuts
Italian ice
Heavy whipping cream

Dairy Products
Eat 2 to 3 servings daily

Meat, poultry, fish and dry beans
Eat 2 to 3 servings daily

Milk—8 ozs.
Yogurt—8 ozs.
Gelato—$\frac{1}{2}$ cup
Ricotta cheese—$\frac{1}{2}$ cup
Mozzarella cheese—1 $\frac{1}{2}$ ozs.

Veal—2-3 ozs.
Beef—2-3 ozs.
Squid—2-3 ozs.
Sausage—2-3 ozs.
Beans—$\frac{1}{2}$ cup
Lentils—$\frac{1}{2}$ cup
Luncheon meats—2-3 ozs.

Vegetables
Eat 3 to 5 servings daily

Eggplant—$\frac{1}{2}$ cup
Spinach—$\frac{1}{2}$ cup
Artichoke—$\frac{1}{2}$ cup
Mushrooms—$\frac{1}{2}$ cup
Marinara sauce—$\frac{1}{2}$ cup
Green or red pepper—$\frac{1}{2}$ cup

Dried figs—2
Grapefruit—$\frac{1}{2}$
Pomegranate—1
Blueberries—$\frac{1}{2}$ cup
Raspberries—$\frac{1}{2}$ cup

Fruits
Eat 2 to 4 servings daily

Grains
Eat 6 to 11 servings daily

Polenta—$\frac{1}{2}$ cup
Risotto—$\frac{1}{2}$ cup
Linguine—$\frac{1}{2}$ cup
Spaghetti—$\frac{1}{2}$ cup

Gnocchi—$\frac{1}{2}$ cup
Bread sticks—2
Italian bread—1 slice

Meals and Menus (cont.)

Mexican Fare

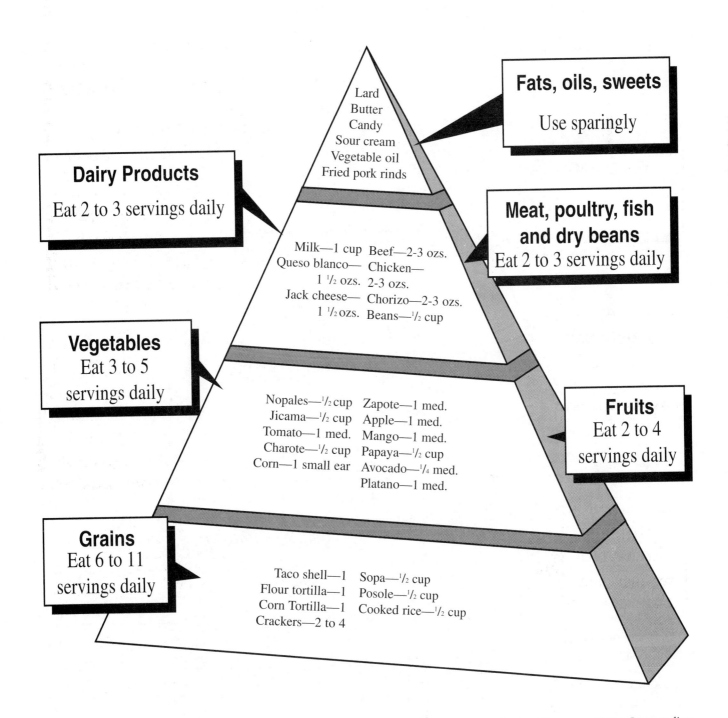

Fats, oils, sweets
Use sparingly

Lard
Butter
Candy
Sour cream
Vegetable oil
Fried pork rinds

Dairy Products
Eat 2 to 3 servings daily

Meat, poultry, fish and dry beans
Eat 2 to 3 servings daily

Milk—1 cup   Beef—2-3 ozs.
Queso blanco—   Chicken—
  1 ½ ozs.   2-3 ozs.
Jack cheese—   Chorizo—2-3 ozs.
  1 ½ ozs.   Beans—½ cup

Vegetables
Eat 3 to 5
servings daily

Nopales—½ cup   Zapote—1 med.
Jicama—½ cup   Apple—1 med.
Tomato—1 med.   Mango—1 med.
Charote—½ cup   Papaya—½ cup
Corn—1 small ear Avocado—¼ med.
                 Platano—1 med.

Fruits
Eat 2 to 4
servings daily

Grains
Eat 6 to 11
servings daily

Taco shell—1   Sopa—½ cup
Flour tortilla—1 Posole—½ cup
Corn Tortilla—1   Cooked rice—½ cup
Crackers—2 to 4

Meals and Menus *(cont.)*

Now that you have studied the food pyramids and thought about your own food choices, consider the kinds of meals a main character in your story might like. From what you know about that character, plan a typical meal and show it in the chart below. Be sure to write the specific foods in the correct sections and label the pyramid with your character's name. Share your chart with classmates.

Story _____ Character _____

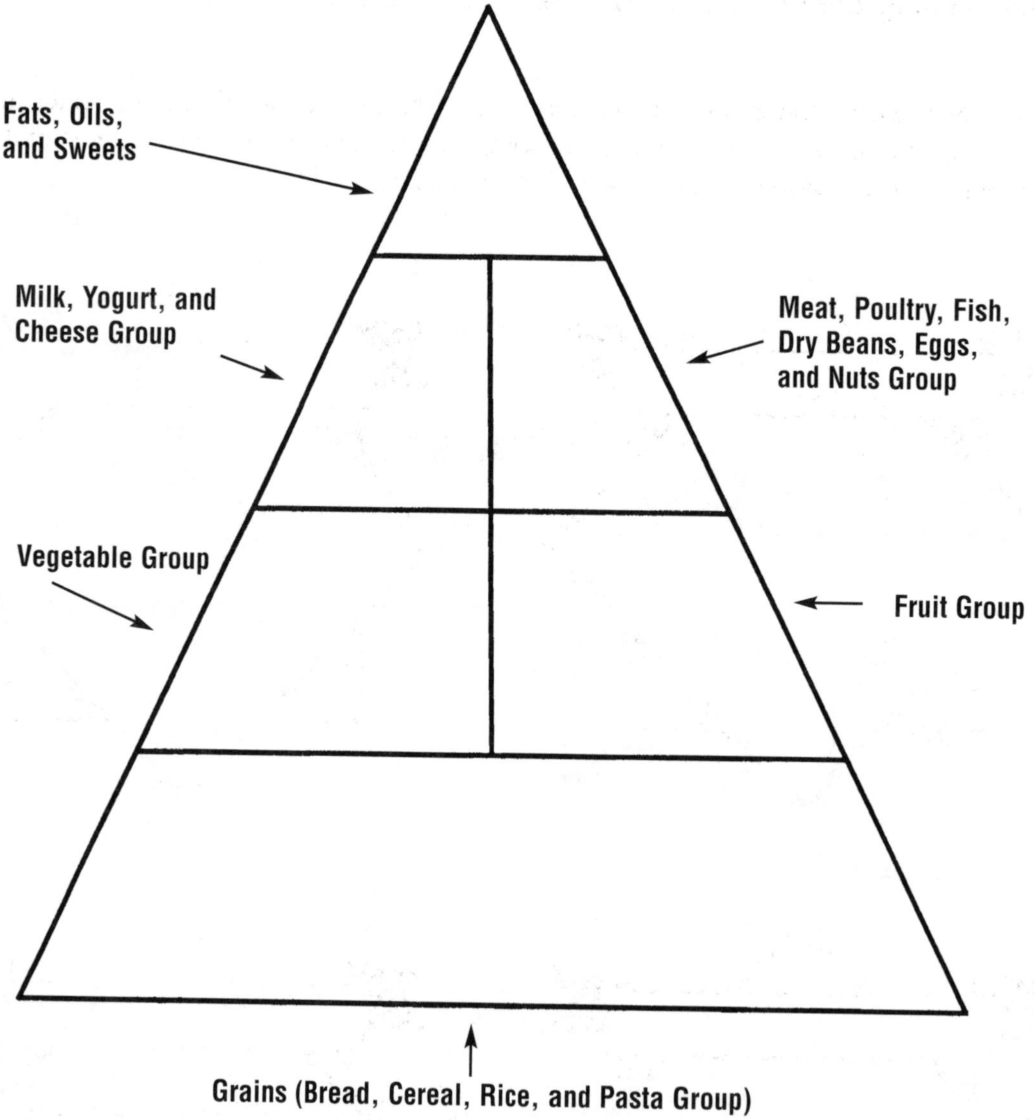

Fats, Oils,
and Sweets

Milk, Yogurt, and
Cheese Group

Meat, Poultry, Fish,
Dry Beans, Eggs,
and Nuts Group

Vegetable Group

Fruit Group

Grains (Bread, Cereal, Rice, and Pasta Group)

Do you think your character is eating healthful meals? _____

Explain why. _____

_____

If not, what would you recommend that the character change in the daily menu? (Name specific foods to add or subtract.) _____

_____

Mottos

A motto is a word or phrase that describes a principle that someone lives by. Here are some examples.

- **To thine own self be true.**
- **Haste makes waste.**
- **Do not judge a person until you have walked a mile in his moccasins.**
- **Never pass by the chance to do a kindness, for you may never pass the same way again.**

Create mottos for four characters in your book or story. Place the name of your character in the banner at the top of a square below and write the motto within the borders of the square. Be sure that the motto you create is one that the character would truly want to live by.

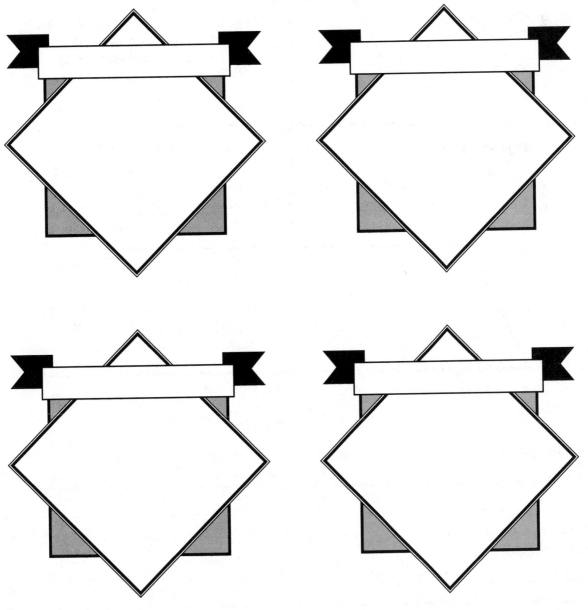

Codes!

Throughout the ages—from ancient petroglyphs to Egyptian hieroglyphics to modern international telegraphy—people have developed many different ways of communicating with **sounds, gestures**, and **written symbols**. If a set of signals is special or is designed to be known by a special group, it is often called a **code**. Developing and understanding codes helps us to understand how communication and languages work.

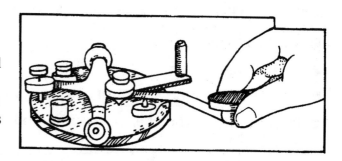

You and your classmates will make a class code. First, write your own ideas for the code below. Then, share your ideas with the class. Together, everyone can choose the best ideas and make a class code chart. To help, your teacher can write the ideas on the chalkboard, and the class can vote. "Speak" with this code as much as you can for one week in class!

Message	Your Code
Thank you.	_____
Please.	_____
I am thirsty.	_____
I am hungry.	_____
I am tired.	_____
I am happy.	_____
I am sad.	_____
Be quiet!	_____
May I sharpen my pencil?	_____
Open your book.	_____
Close your book.	_____
Your homework is . . .	_____
It is time to eat.	_____
It is time to exercise.	_____
It is time to go home.	_____

Think of one more message and the code for it.

Message: _____

Code: _____

Codes! *(cont.)*

Suppose you had to communicate without making a sound! Practice reading and making the letters of the manual alphabet found on pages 46 and 47. After you have become familiar with the position of the letters, try to translate the message below.

Write your answer to the coded message on the lines below each sign.

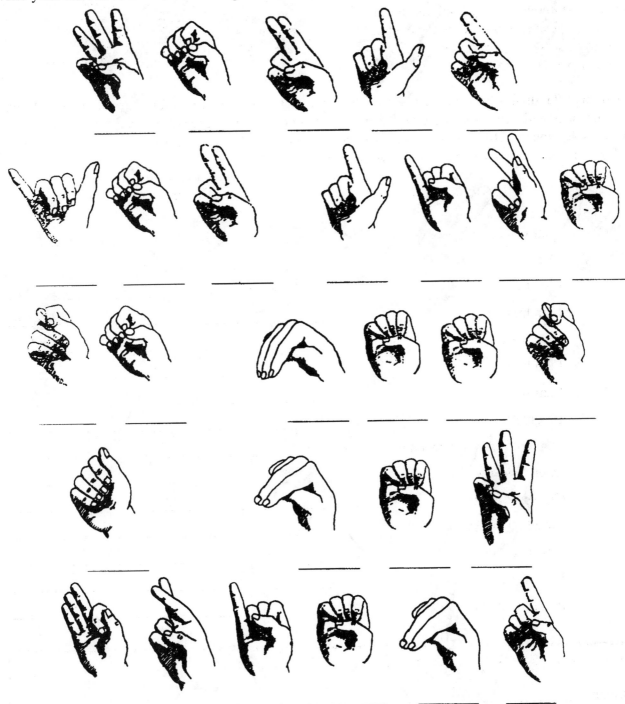

Can you make this same message into your hand? If you could not see, could you learn to "feel" each letter? Close your eyes and try it!

Codes! *(cont.)*

The Manual Alphabet, A–M

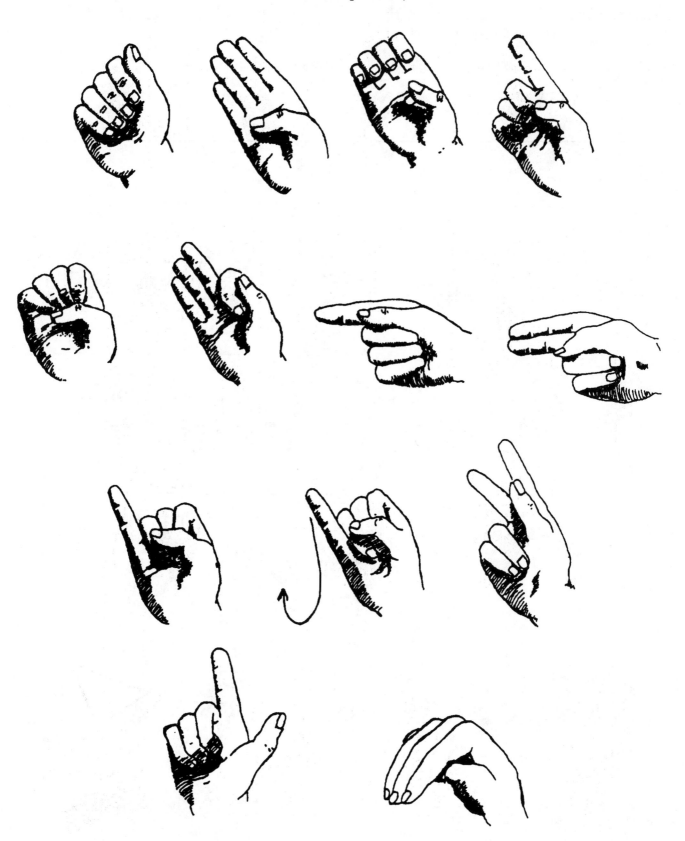

Codes! *(cont.)*

The Manual Alphabet N–Z

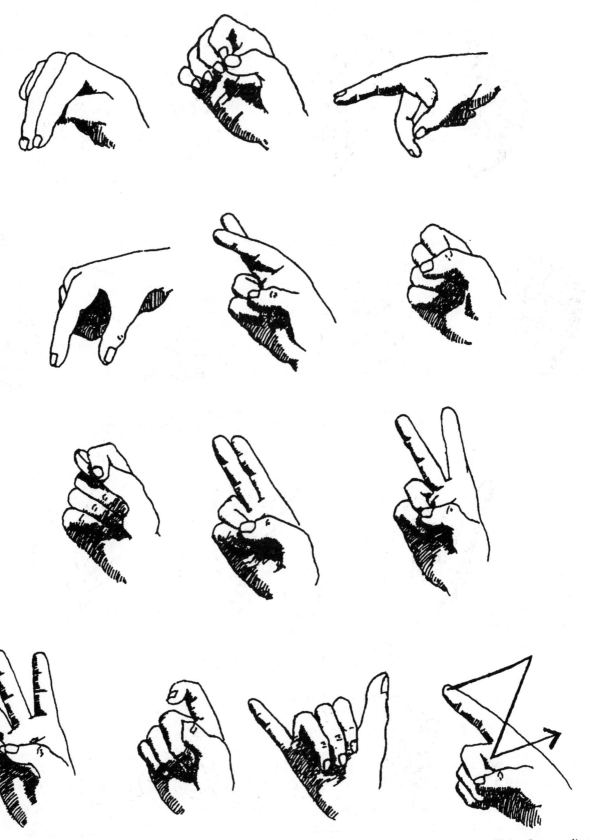

Codes! *(cont.)*

Following is a code based on the "wingding" (sometimes called "dingbat") font of a computer program.

A—✡ a—❁ B—✢ b—❂ C—✤ c—✳

D—♣ d—❄ E—✤ e—❄ F—◆ f—❄

G—◈ g—✳ H—★ h—✴ I—☆ i—❋

J—✪ j—✳ K—☆ k—✳ L—✮ l—●

M—✭ m—○ N—✩ n—■ O—✯ o—❑

P—☆ p—❐ Q—✳ q—❑ R—✴ r—❒

S—✳ s—▲ T—✳ t—▼ U—✳ u—◆

V—✦ v—❖ W—✳ w—◗ X—✳ x—❘

Y—✺ y—❙ Z—✺ z—∎

Using your computer at home or one in your school, write the following messages in wingding code. Be sure to follow the code as shown above.

- ■ The name of the book (story) I just read.

- ■ The name of the author.

- ■ The name of my favorite character.

Challenge: Set up a different wingding code of your own and send a message to another student in the class, at the same time giving a decoded copy to your teacher. Then see if the other student can "crack" your code.

Animal or Human?

Many stories about animals or featuring animals demonstrate the abilities of some animals to do astonishing things. Sometimes they may seem almost capable of being human. In other cases, of course, they may possess characteristics that are *beyond* human abilities.

Considering the animal in the story you are reading (or have just finished reading), list 10 characteristics that are *similar* to those of humans.

1. _____
2. _____
3. _____
4. _____
5. _____
6. _____
7. _____
8. _____
9. _____
10. _____

Now list 10 characteristics that are *different* from those of humans.

1. _____
2. _____
3. _____
4. _____
5. _____
6. _____
7. _____
8. _____
9. _____
10. _____

Name one thing that humans can do that animals cannot. _____

_____

Money

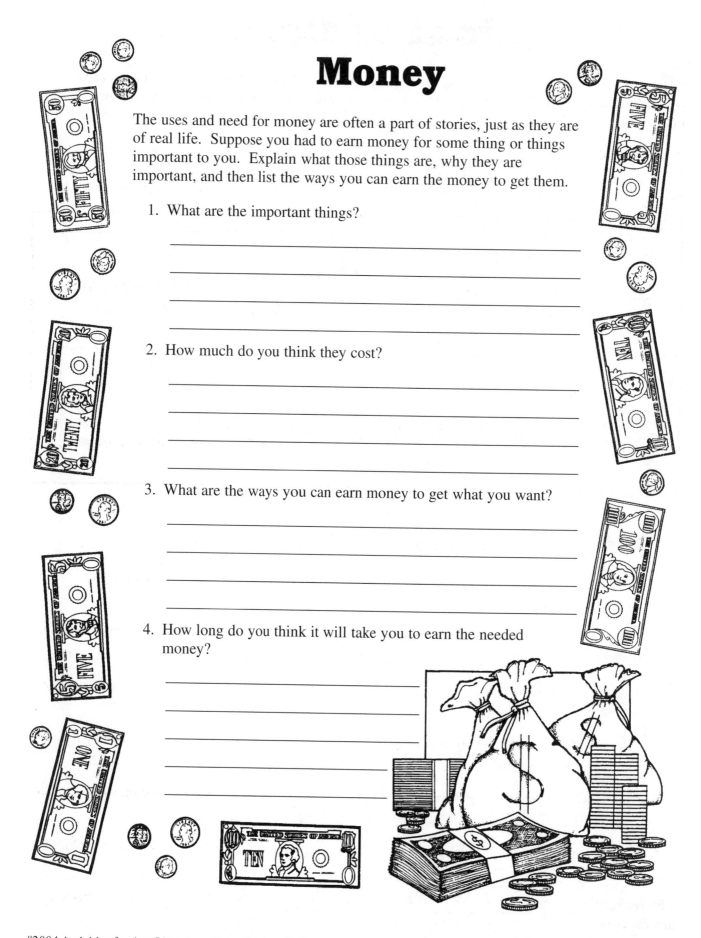

The uses and need for money are often a part of stories, just as they are of real life. Suppose you had to earn money for some thing or things important to you. Explain what those things are, why they are important, and then list the ways you can earn the money to get them.

1. What are the important things?

_____

_____

_____

_____

2. How much do you think they cost?

_____

_____

_____

_____

3. What are the ways you can earn money to get what you want?

_____

_____

_____

_____

4. How long do you think it will take you to earn the needed money?

_____

_____

_____

_____

Word Power!

Some authors are very artistic, painting word pictures in rich detail. They leave us with powerful memories of the scenes they describe and the people whose lives they create. Among the literary devices used by such writers are *imagery, simile, personification,* and *paradox.*

Read the following excerpts from one story. Underline examples of imagery, circle all similes, draw a box around any personification, and put brackets around the paradox. Use the definitions in the box to help you with your analysis. Sometimes, more than one literary device may be used in an example.

Imagery: vivid description appealing to any or all of the five senses	Simile: comparison between two dissimilar things, using like or as
Personification: giving inanimate objects human characteristics	Paradox: self-contradictory statement that is nevertheless somehow true

1. "... the sun sank like stone into the purple sea."

2. "They began to relax, listening to the sound-filled silence."

3. "The still afternoon stood poised on tiptoe, holding its breath for the crack of thunder and following downpour."

4. "Like foam on a painted wave, the delicate blossoms dusted the surface of the low grass near the stream."

5. "... three armchairs and an old rocker stood stiffly in the room, like strangers at a party, uneasy and silent."

6. "The prairie they crossed was humming with the drone of bees, and grasshoppers jumped before them as if springs in the earth were flipping them up miniature kangaroos."

7. "The clouds spread apart, and the sky opened up its dazzling blue like an unfolding silken curtain, shimmering with light and power till she became dizzy."

8. "Like colors spilled from a paintbox, the evening sky spread out in pools of shining red and pink and orange, curling and darkening around the edges."

Challenge: Find some examples of these literary devices in your story and write them on the back of this paper or on another sheet of paper.

Values to Live By

Note to the teacher: *Before duplicating this activity, write in the names of the characters you select on the appropriate blanks.*

Read the list of values in the box below. Rank them in order of importance according to how the different characters in your story would act. Number 1 equals the most important, and number 5 equals the least important.

| pride | honesty | wealth | kindness | loyalty |

Rank these values the way _____ would.

1. _____   2. _____   3. _____   4. _____   5. _____

Rank these values the way _____ would.

1. _____   2. _____   3. _____   4. _____   5. _____

Rank these values the way _____ would.

1. _____   2. _____   3. _____   4. _____   5. _____

Rank these values the way _____ would.

1. _____   2. _____   3. _____   4. _____   5. _____

Rank these values the way _____ would.

1. _____   2. _____   3. _____   4. _____   5. _____

Rank these values the way _____ would.

1. _____   2. _____   3. _____   4. _____   5. _____

Rank these values the way _____ would.

1. _____   2. _____   3. _____   4. _____   5. _____

Rank these values the way _____ would.

1. _____   2. _____   3. _____   4. _____   5. _____

Rank these values the way _____ would.

1. _____   2. _____   3. _____   4. _____   5. _____

Rank these values the way _____ would.

1. _____   2. _____   3. _____   4. _____   5. _____

Fantasy or Reality?

Fantasy stories are filled with imaginative writing. However, within fantasies are incidents that really do happen in the real world.

Think of 10 examples of *fantasy* that are described in your story.

1. _____
2. _____
3. _____
4. _____
5. _____
6. _____
7. _____
8. _____
9. _____
10. _____

Think of 10 examples of *reality* that are described in your story.

1. _____
2. _____
3. _____
4. _____
5. _____
6. _____
7. _____
8. _____
9. _____
10. _____

Truth and Fantasy

Note to the teacher: *Before duplicating the activity below, write in the names of the characters you select.*

The story you have read is a fantasy—a story that is not true. However, within every fantasy lies reality—a reality of personalities. Many of the characters in the story act and think *realistically*, just as one of us might do.

For each of the characters named below, give an example of something he or she does or says that could only happen in a fantasy. Then give an example of something done or said that could easily happen in the real world.

_____
Character

fantasy: _____

reality: _____

_____
Character

fantasy: _____

reality: _____

_____
Character

fantasy: _____

reality: _____

_____
Character

fantasy: _____

reality: _____

_____
Character

fantasy: _____

reality: _____

You Choose!

1. What part of the story was the most frightening?

   _____

   _____

   Why? _____

   _____

2. What part of the story was full of the most action?

   _____

   _____

   Why? _____

   _____

3. What part of the story was the saddest?

   _____

   _____

   Why? _____

   _____

4. What part of the story was the most believable?

   _____

   _____

   Why? _____

   _____

5. What part of the story was the most meaningful to you?

   _____

   _____

   Why? _____

   _____

Character

Note to the teacher: *Before duplicating the activity below, fill in the name of the character you select.*

There are many qualities that make up the personality of each individual. These qualities tell us a great deal about the people we really are.

Circle the qualities you think_____ has that make him/her a special person different from others.

courageous	self-pity
sense of humor	brave
disciplined	intelligent
love for family	enthusiastic
selfish	optimistist
hopeful	greedy
pessimistic	friendly
fun-loving	respectful
proud	polite
honest	miserable

Other qualities you may wish to add:

_____   _____   _____

_____   _____   _____

Including your additions to the list above, which qualities do you think helped this person most during the story?_____

Were there any qualities which you think harmed this person during the story? Explain:

_____

_____

_____

Which of the qualities listed above describe your own character? _____

_____

_____

_____

Events and Emotions

What events in the story caused you to feel these emotions?

1. **Fear** _____

   _____

2. **Disgust** _____

   _____

3. **Sadness** _____

   _____

4. **Pity** _____

   _____

5. **Joy** _____

   _____

6. **Hopelessness** _____

   _____

7. **Anger** _____

   _____

8. **Frustration** _____

   _____

9. **Hope** _____

   _____

10. **Worry** _____

   _____

Relationships

Choose one pair of characters from your story and complete the background information for them that is requested in the form below. Explain each answer fully.

Characters: _____

What are these characters likely to do together? _____

_____

What are these characters likely to say to one another? _____

_____

What are these characters likely to think about each other? _____

_____

What is responsible for the type of relationship they have with one another? _____

_____

Does their relationship undergo any kind of change in the course of the story? _____

_____

Is the relationship likely to change in the future? _____

_____

Is their relationship a "good" or "bad" one? _____

_____

On a separate piece of paper, create a dialogue which shows these two characters and their typical interaction. Choose the character you would like to portray. Practice your dialogue and present your role-playing sketch to the class.

Character's name: _____

Played by: _____

Character's name: _____

Played by: _____

Character Profile

Develop one of the main characters of the story into a real person. As you fill in these blanks, try to be in the mind of the characters.

Book_____

Author _____

Name of Character_____

Age_____ Height_____ Weight _____ Male or Female _____

Hair Color _____ Eye Color _____ Skin Color _____

1. Where does he/she live? _____

2. What kind of job does he/she have or would like to have? _____

_____

Why? _____

3. Who is his/her best friend? _____

4. Does he/she have any enemies?_____Who?_____

5. Does he/she like life? Explain. _____

_____

6. Fill in these blanks with his/her favorites.

Color _____ Food _____

Animal_____ Hobby _____

Sport _____ Music_____

Place to go _____

Thing to do _____

7. Would you like to have this character as a friend? _____

Explain._____

_____

_____

_____

_____

_____

_____

The Hero

What is your definition of a *hero*?

_____

_____

What are a few deeds you think a typical hero might do?

_____

_____

_____

How is the hero in your book like a typical one?

_____

_____

_____

How is he/she unlike a typical hero?

_____

_____

_____

What kinds of heroic things do you think he/she might do if living in your time or neighborhood?

_____

_____

_____

What are some of the heroic characteristics he/she has that you also have?

_____

_____

_____

Name three people you know who have the capacity to become the type of hero he/she was in your story. Explain each of your choices.

1. _____ reason: _____

   _____

2. _____ reason: _____

   _____

3. _____ reason: _____

   _____

Compare and Contrast

Some stories have been made into movies, available at most video rental stores. After reading a book, view the movie with your class. Compare and contrast the book and the movie.

The book and the movie are different in these ways:

_____

_____

_____

_____

The book and the movie are the same in these ways:

_____

_____

_____

_____

I like the_____better because_____

_____

_____

_____

Significant Scenes

Every story has certain special scenes that are memorable and important to advance the action (the plot development). Which scenes do you feel are the most significant for your story?

Work with a partner to select five of those scenes and create an accordion book that presents them in order.

Directions for making an accordion book:

1. Cut six pieces of tagboard the same size and shape. You may choose any size or shape that can contain writing, illustrations, and be connected at the side edges.

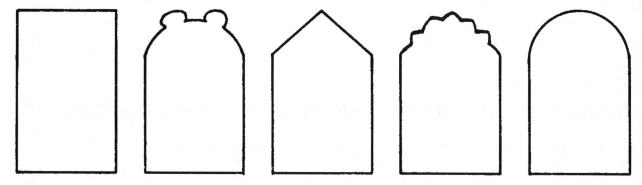

2. Tape the six pieces of tagboard together at the sides. (Put tape on both front and back.)

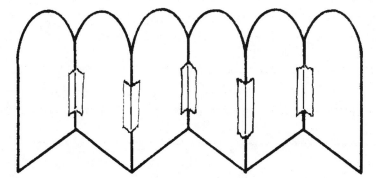

3. Design a cover for your book and illustrate the significant scenes you have selected. You may draw directly on the tagboard or on separate paper to be glued into the book.

4. Write a brief synopsis of each scene on the appropriate book page.

5. Display your accordion book for the class!

Sequel

You have been chosen to write a sequel (Part II) for the book you have just finished reading. Fill in the blanks below. Then write an explanation of what will happen in your new book.

Title of the book you read: _____

Author: _____

Title of the new book you will write: _____

_____

Your name: _____

Setting (time and location) of the new book: _____

_____

Is this the same setting as in Part I?_____Explain: _____

_____

_____

Protagonist (main character) of the new book: _____

Description of the protagonist: _____

_____

Is this the same protagonist as in Part I?_____Explain: _____

_____

_____

Antagonist (person or thing causing conflict for the protagonist) of the new book:

_____

Description of antagonist:_____

_____

Is this the same antagonist as in Part I?_____Explain: _____

_____

What are some things that are the same in each book? _____

_____

What are some things that are different in each book? _____

_____

On the back of this page or on another sheet of paper, write an explanation of what will happen in your new book. Share your ideas with your class.

Now What?

You have just finished the last page of your book. You want MORE! If you could have the author write a sequel of your choice, what would you want in the new book? Write him/her a letter with your advice!

_____ (date)

Dear _____

I have just finished reading _____ and enjoyed it very much. I would like to give you some of my ideas for its sequel.

The name of the new book should be _____

_____

In your new book, please include these things:

_____

_____

_____

_____

_____

I believe the strongest ending for this new book would be _____

_____

_____

_____

_____

Thank you for reading my advice. Let me know if you like my ideas.

Sincerely,

_____

Other Worlds, Other Times

Would you like to create your own magical world like professional writers do? That, of course, is what all writers do—whether they tell stories of "fantasy" or "reality."

Work with a partner. Pretend that you are from another world. Make a scrapbook of your world that includes the items on the checklist below. You may include other items, also. After you have completed your world scrapbook, share it with your class.

Include these things in your scrapbook:

❑   1. a scrapbook cover with the name of your world, a drawing of it, and your names

❑   2. a brief, one-page description of how you discovered your world

❑   3. the age and location of your world

❑   4. a detailed map of your world

❑   5. an introduction to the inhabitants of your world

❑   6. an explanation of the friendliness (or unfriendliness) of the inhabitants

❑   7. drawings of the inhabitants

❑   8. drawings of the homes of the inhabitants

❑   9. conflicts that the inhabitants may have

❑ 10. a one-day diary entry by you during your time there

❑ 11. a description of your part in this world

❑ 12. an explanation of your future in this world (Will you stay or leave? Are you, or will you, always be welcome?)

❑ 13. _____

❑ 14. _____

❑ 15. _____

❑ 16. _____

❑ 17. _____

Other Worlds, Other Times *(cont.)*

Complete this map of your new world. Then cut it out and paste the map in your scrapbook.

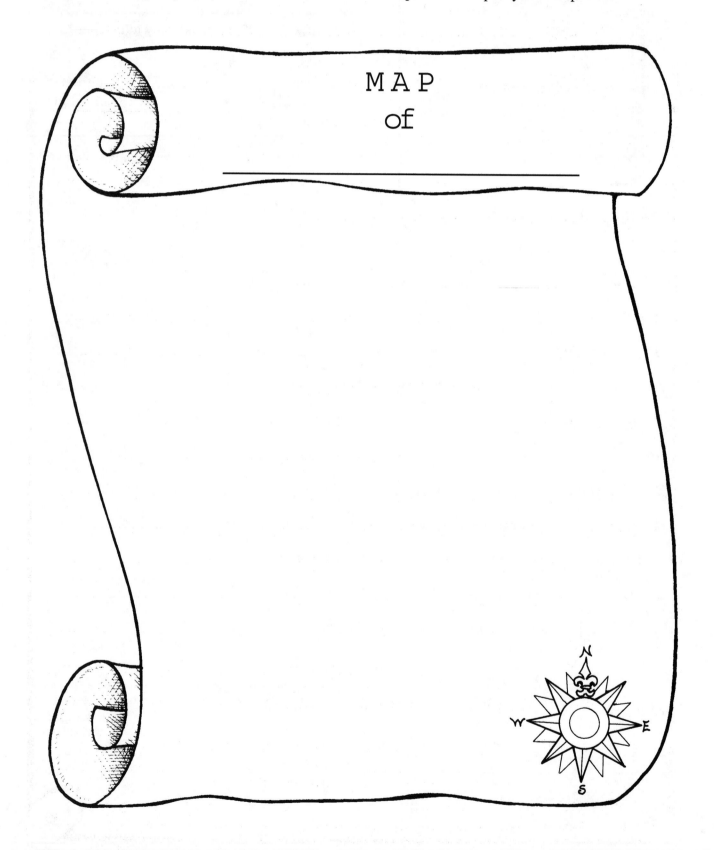

Other Worlds, Other Times *(cont.)*

Complete this cast-of-characters list, naming and describing the characters in your world. Then cut it out and paste the list in your scrapbook.

Cast of Characters

The ruler of_____is_____.

Description:_____

_____

_____

The being we first meet in_____is_____.

Description:_____

_____

_____

These are the characters who uphold the good in our world: _____

_____

_____

Descriptions: _____

_____

These are the characters who cause trouble in our world: _____

_____

_____

Descriptions: _____

_____

_____

_____

Other Worlds, Other Times *(cont.)*

Work together with your partner(s) to create a song that tells of your newly created world. Begin by writing your own ideas for a song here. Also, suggest an idea of a melody by naming a familiar one, tape recording a new one, or performing one for your class!

Share all your song ideas and create a song worthy of the inhabitants of your world.

A Gift of Age

Many stories feature people of all ages—children, adults, grandparents, and even great-grandparents. One of the best ways to learn about other people and other times is to interview those people.

Interview a person who is at least old enough to be your grandparent. Use the ideas below to help you in your interview. Use all the starred topics and at least five of the topics that are not starred. Write down each interview question you ask and the response your person gives. Put your written interview pages together and create "A Gift of Age" cover.

Suggested Interview Topics

Childhood: Tell me about . . .

- ★ what the world was like
- ★ your time with your family
- ★ grade school experiences
- your hero
- ★ a typical day
- ★ where you lived
- your favorite music

- ★ what you did for fun
- your pets
- your favorite teacher
- ★ your dreams
- ★ your special friends
- ★ your responsibilities

Teen Years: Tell me about . . .

- ★ your first date
- ★ your first job
- ★ your special friends
- a typical day
- your first drive

- your most embarrassing moment
- ★ what you did for fun
- ★ your responsibilities
- ★ your special interests
- ★ your dreams

Adulthood: Tell me about . . .

- ★ your jobs
- ★ your children (if any)
- ★ your special friends
- ★ your military service
- ★ a great sorrow
- ★ a great joy
- ★ what you do best
- ★ advice you have for living the best life a person can

- ★ your marriage
- your grandchildren (if any)
- how the world has changed
- your food likes and dislikes
- ★ your view of the world
- a favorite poem or story
- ★ hobbies or special interests

Travel Brochure

Pretend you are an advertising person for the businesses in the area where your story takes place. You are interested in attracting tourists to your part of the country. Make a travel brochure for your area, describing such a trip in exciting and colorful ways. Anything in the setting or the story itself—landscape, natural resources, yearly events, activities, festivals, etc.—may be included.

Here are some ideas to help you in the making of your travel brochure. Do not hesitate to use ideas of your own.

1. Make an "accordion fold."
   (You may use front and back.)

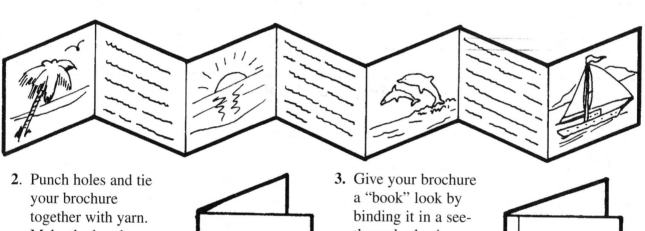

2. Punch holes and tie your brochure together with yarn. Make the brochure "homey" looking.

3. Give your brochure a "book" look by binding it in a see-through plastic cover with a slip-on binding.

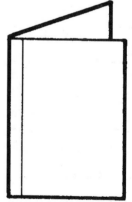

4. Create a many-fold single sheet presentation with the brochure opening to a gigantic picture that will make the travelers want to go—NOW!

 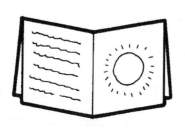  

Justify!

You have been asked to decide if your book is a story that really could have happened.

Reasons This Story Could Have Happened

_____

_____

_____

_____

_____

_____

Reasons This Story Could Not Have Happened

_____

_____

_____

_____

_____

_____

You now have to make a choice: Could this story actually have happened?

_____

Justify the reasons for your decision. _____

_____

_____

The Characters and You

Consider all of the characters in the story as you answer the questions on this page.

1. Which character would you be most likely to admire?

   _____

   Why? _____

   _____

2. Which character would you be most likely to dislike?

   _____

   Why? _____

   _____

3. Which character would you be most likely to befriend?

   _____

   Why? _____

   _____

4. Which character would you be most likely to learn from?

   _____

   Why? _____

   _____

   _____

5. Which character would you be most likely to write a book, song, or movie about?_____

   Why? _____

   _____

6. Which character would you like to know more about?

   _____

   Why? _____

   _____

Heroism

Heroism can encompass many actions. For some, great acts of heroism may be telling the truth, touching a snake, standing up for what you believe, or completing a homework assignment. Being a hero can even mean saying "no" to your friends if they ask you to do something you know is wrong.

1. What is heroism to you?_____

_____

_____

2. Which of the characters in your book do you consider to be heroic?

_____

_____

3. Select the most heroic character in the book and explain your choice.

_____

_____

_____

4. Write one example of something you did, even though you were afraid to do it. _____

_____

_____

5. Write one example of a time you told the truth when it would have been easier to lie._____

_____

_____

6. Write one example of a time you helped someone else without thinking of yourself._____

_____

_____

7. Write one example of a time you said "no" to a friend because what this friend was doing was wrong. _____

_____

_____

8. Are you a hero?_____

Changes

Note to the teacher: *Fill in the blank lines with specific character names that you select for the students to discuss.*

When characters in a story learn from their experiences, they grow as people. Sometimes this growth makes them change the way they are and what they do.

1. What does _____ learn in the story that makes him change as a person?

   _____

   _____

2. What does _____ learn in the story that makes her change as a person?

   _____

   _____

3. What did you learn from the story that might help you change as a person?

   _____

   _____

   _____

4. Do you think it is realistic for characters to change as time passes, or is it more realistic for them to stay the same?

   _____

   Why? _____

   _____

   _____

   _____

Is It Right or Wrong?

Almost all stories tell of happenings that are "right" and happenings that are "wrong." Select two right events and two wrong events from your story and describe them in the books below. Explain in the lines below each book why you think it is right or wrong.

Right   **Wrong**

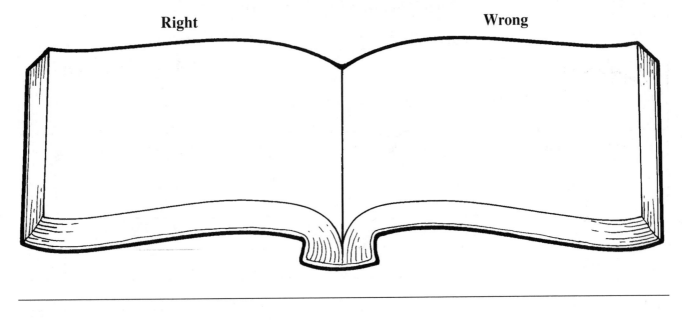

_____

_____

_____

Right   **Wrong**

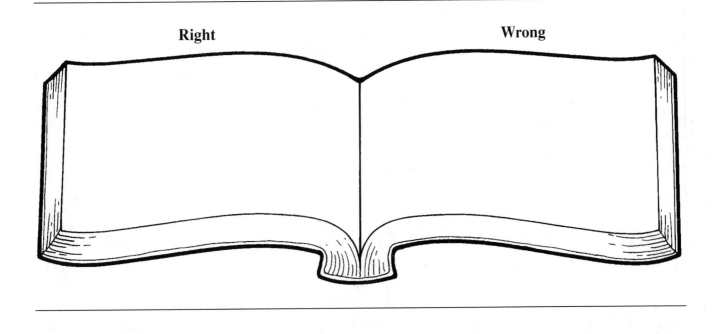

_____

_____

_____

Friendship

Good books often tell of friendship between characters. Following are two lists—one that tells of things that often *bring* friends together and one that tells of qualities that often *keep* friends together.

Things That Bring Friends Together

- neighborhood
- sports
- parents
- books
- scouts

- age
- hobbies
- pets
- school
- toys

Write each thing on the list below in the order of its importance to you (#1 is the most important).

1. _____
2. _____
3. _____
4. _____
5. _____

6. _____
7. _____
8. _____
9. _____
10. _____

Name two friends from your book and tell what brought them together.

_____

_____

Qualities That Keep Friends Together

- funny
- athletic
- quiet
- understanding
- smart

- brave
- creative
- loyal
- honest
- loving

Write each quality on the list below in the order of its importance to you (#1 is the most important).

1. _____
2. _____
3. _____
4. _____
5. _____

6. _____
7. _____
8. _____
9. _____
10. _____

On the back of this paper, write which qualities on the list you think were important to the friendship of the two characters in your book. Tell why you chose these qualities.

"Q and A"

This is a stimulating, cooperative-learning-based game which employs all levels of Bloom's Taxonomy skills. The dynamics of the game are such that all students can participate successfully and are engaged at all times. Play "Q and A" before administering tests, or use this activity as an assessment form itself. There are a number of ways to play the game, and as you run through "Q and A" a few times, you will probably want to customize the game to best suit your needs and the needs of your students.

Materials

- standard-size tagboard
- 25 self-adhesive pockets (the kind used in library books for check-out cards)
- 25 colored circle stickers—5 each of 5 different colors
- 25 index cards (to fit into library pockets)
- 6 rulers or 1-foot (30 cm) sticks like paint stirrers
- 6 different-colored oval shapes with 10-inch (25 cm) diameters
- colored markers

Set-up of Game Board

1. Place the pockets on the tagboard to form five rows of five, and then stick the backs to the tagboard.
2. Determine which color each row will be.
3. Starting with the first row (horizontally), place one color of the sticker circles on the upper, front part of the pocket card. Continue placing stickers on all five of the top row of pockets.
4. Determine the colors for the next rows and repeat the process until the entire board represents five different-colored rows of pockets with dots.
5. Starting with the top row again, use an ink marker in the same color as the stickers to write a large number "10" on each of the cards.
6. Use the same procedure but with different numbers for the next four rows, using matching ink markers for the respective dots.

Game Board suggestions:
Laminate the board, with the pockets glued on, for durability. Use a razor blade to cut open the pockets.

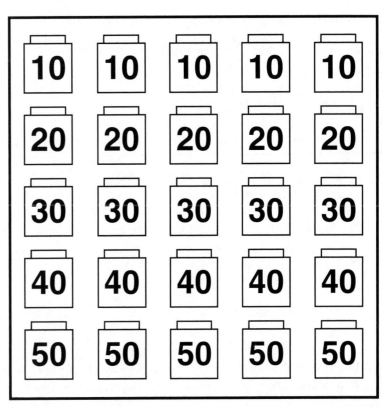

"Q and A" *(cont.)*

How to Play

■ Arrange the students into six groups of five or whatever works for your class numbers.

■ Place the game sticks at each table.

■ On the board, write down the six different colors for each group for score-keeping purposes.

■ Begin with one group and rotate in a clockwise fashion.

■ Each team member will have an opportunity to hold the game stick. Even though team members collaborate on the answers and decisions that need to be made, only the person holding the game stick is allowed to speak for the group. The game stick is then rotated clockwise after each team's turn.

■ The game show host or hostess will ask that team to decide which color card and point value they wish to try. The host then reads the card aloud for the whole class to hear. Give the team about one minute to discuss possible answers. While this team is thinking, the other teams should also be doing the same, since they may have an opportunity to answer this question at a later time.

■ The game-stick holder will then answer the question. If the answer is correct, that team receives the points, and the game then moves on to the next team. If the team does not answer the question correctly, then the next team in the rotation has a chance to steal the points.

■ If the next team answers the previous question correctly, they get the points for that card and then may also choose another card to answer. If the second team cannot answer the "steal" question, then the card simply goes back into its place, and they still get to choose a question.

■ This procedure continues throughout the course of the game until all the cards have been answered.

Rules and Guidelines

■ Only the person holding the game stick may speak for the group.

■ All responses to questions must be discussed with the entire group before answering. If the game stick holder speaks before collaboration, then the team loses its turn.

■ The majority of the team must agree on the response before it is presented to the host or hostess.

■ Teams may respond only when it is their turn.

"Q and A" *(cont.)*

Set-up of "Game Sticks"

1. Write "Q and A" in large print on each of the colored oval shapes.

2. Laminate the shapes for durability.

3. Tape or glue each shape to a stick or ruler to make a sign. (See illustration.)

Set-up of Game Cards

1. The questions for "Q and A" range from easy to challenging. Any 10-point questions are at the Bloom's knowledge level, beginning with "Who," "When," or "What." The 50-point questions will adhere to the Synthesis and Evaluation levels, asking students to modify, judge, classify, and evaluate. (A suggested questioning chart according to Bloom's Taxonomy is included on page 80.)

2. With the card held lengthwise, write the point value at the top. On the back of the card, write the question at the top and the answer at the bottom.

3. Place the cards in their appropriate pocket slot with the point value showing. (See illustration.)

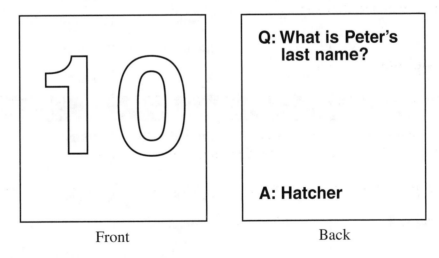

Front   Back

Object of Game

The object of "Q and A" is to be the team with the most points at the end of the game. Teams take turns answering the questions, with each member of each team also having a turn to speak. The game is finished when all the cards have been answered correctly.

"Q and A" *(cont.)*

Some Helpful Hints!

■ The questions may be created by the teacher or by the students.

■ You may want to provide the option of "bonus" cards. Behind one or two cards, place a "bonus" card which provides another question and opportunity for points.

■ Play the game in a Jeopardy style where the host reads the answer, and the students must come up with the possible question.

■ To promote good listening skills, the host or hostess should read the question only two times. This encourages the students to repeat the question to each other.

■ If you will be offering prizes for the winners, be sure to offer a prize to the teams who worked well cooperatively. Competition is fun and necessary, but use every opportunity to affirm successful teamwork.

Bloom's Verbs

Knowledge		Comprehension		Application	
Name	Recall	Explain	Paraphrase	Transfer	Apply
List	Draw	Summarize	Review	Compute	Show
Define	Count	Interpret	Demonstrate	Produce	Change
Match	Identify	Predict	Conclude	Choose	Paint
Label	Sequence	Tell	Generalize	Use	Select
Describe	Quote	Discuss	Locate	Demonstrate	Prepare
Recite	Write	Restate	Identify	Interview	Dramatize
Tell	Find	Illustrate	Report	Draw	Imitate
Analysis		**Synthesis**		**Evaluation**	
Differentiate	Compare	Create	Produce	Judge	Predict
Contrast	Outline	Design	Compose	Select	Rate
Deduce	Characterize	Propose	Invent	Prove	Choose
Classify	Separate	Organize	Pretend	Decide	Evaluate
Debate	Analyze	Construct	Originate	Appraise	Conclude
Research	Discriminate	Develop	Integrate	Rank	Assess
Distinguish	Examine	Plan	Rewrite	Criticize	Justify
Relate	Diagram	Make up	Perform	Prioritize	Argue